# THE PERILS
## OF THE
# YOUNG
# BLACKS

# THE PERILS OF THE YOUNG BLACKS

## DANIEL IYEKS

ARCHWAY
PUBLISHING

Archway Publishing books may be ordered through booksellers or by contacting:

Archway Publishing
1663 Liberty Drive
Bloomington, IN 47403
www.archwaypublishing.com
1 (888) 242-5904

ISBN: 978-1-4808-1911-5 (sc)
ISBN: 978-1-4808-1912-2 (e)

Library of Congress Control Number: 2015943717

Print information available on the last page.

Archway Publishing rev. date: 06/09/2015

# CONTENTS

Preface ...........................................................................vii

Chapter 1   Parental Involvement ...............................1
Chapter 2   Environmental Influence ..........................9
Chapter 3   Black Culture .........................................15
Chapter 4   Schools ..................................................26
Chapter 5   Higher Education ...................................31
Chapter 6   Financial Management ...........................36
Chapter 7   Life Choices ..........................................44
Chapter 8   Capitalism and Fairness .........................48
Chapter 9   Black-on-Black Destruction ...................55
Chapter 10 Discrimination and Racism .....................62
Chapter 11 Family Structures ...................................69

References .......................................................................75
Author Biography ...........................................................77

# PREFACE

It is interesting to hear critics making comments on a Monday morning about how a quarterback should have played a football game despite the fact that they have never handled a ball or played the game. This analogy holds true for anyone trying to solve the problems that young blacks face without themselves being black.

To be accurate in this type of judgment, the critic has to be black, just like the author of this book is, to have grown up where most blacks did, to have attended schools that blacks attend, to raise black children, and to live with them twenty-four hours a day just as the author of this book has done for over fifty years.

Some young blacks are born into difficulties with little or nothing to eat or to hope for. Some move from shelter to shelter. It's like they are starting a two-hundred–meter race from the starting point while their white counterparts start ten meters from the finish line.

The young black hopes to finish at least at the same time the white finishes. This is why most black parents tell their children that they have to work twice as hard and as long as white children to be equally as successful. The reasons for this situation are numerous and will be discussed in detail in this book. Most young blacks' obstacles are there because of the system, racism, and greed, and a few have been placed by the blacks themselves. Even the few for which the blacks could be blamed may be attributed to a lack of early and adequate education for young blacks.

It is quite clear that many progressive blacks who have moved out of the ghetto and into the suburbs may resent the contents of this book, but it has been written to address the misfortunes confronting the underprivileged blacks. It is not for the other blacks who, because of pride, have refused to discuss them.

# CHAPTER 1

## Parental Involvement

Young chimpanzees emulate the behaviors of their parents. Human children do the same. For example, a young black child will emulate the behavior of his or her parents, as will a young white child.

The term *education* is usually defined as the knowledge and training gained from going to school or to college. But true education is usually obtained from parents; it is the training children get to survive in the environment in which they live. Many also think that to be literate is to be educated. This is not so, as can be shown in observing those who we in Western civilization think are primitive; they survive and manage their unindustrialized farming without knowing how to read or write. The slaves of the eighteenth century could not read or write but were efficient in their farming methods. Some of the family farmers of today are well versed and knowledgeable about faming and yet unable to read or write. Literacy does, however, enhance the ability to express oneself.

The unfortunate problem in black neighborhoods is that some

young blacks who are having children are hardly educated, even when they are certified to be literate by the public schools. Some young blacks without parental attention and without goals or inspiration from their elders are forced to listen to self-made bullies and advisors in the streets who tell them that "quick and easy going" is the order of life. The critics will say that parents need not be educated to motivate their children because they are working hard daily to provide for their children. The dedication of the parents is great, but their know-how may not be enough.

These bullies or advisors—who often are less educated than the young blacks—declare the streets' rules and the commandments for all to follow. After a young black has heard these voices for years, his thoughts become the same as those of his uneducated mentors, and he begins to act and follow the rules of the streets. In homes where educated parents, including farmers and blue-collar parents, discipline their children, the young black children are prevented from reaching the streets and listening to the street lords and barons. In most cases, the best way to educate children is to start teaching them early to listen to and to respect their parents. In such cases, the children are more likely to listen to their parents' advice when they become adults.

The young blacks who master the streets believe that they have arrived and regard themselves as adults. While they are adults according to their ages, mentally they are still children without goals or focus. The lack of educated and literate parents has deprived these young blacks of the ability to focus and to achieve goals.

The strong, active street men gravitate to young women, or the young women gravitate to them because of their looks or their physical build. (This conclusion was reached after discussing the issue with young blacks on and off the streets.) These young men and women are physically adults, but they are unprepared for the challenges of the society in which they live. Many young blacks become sexually active without taking the necessary precautions and without the sexual education required to avoid contracting sexually transmitted diseases and causing pregnancies, which is common among all races. Some people preach abstinence before marriage. Such preaching will work with young blacks from educated homes when the pros and cons of early sexual involvement are thoroughly explained.

In some cases, the sexual involvement between two young adults does not end with the presumed pleasure but with an unplanned and unwanted pregnancy, in addition to other health issues as indicated statistically by the teenage pregnancy rates in the United States. Then, a young black man—though seen as big and bad on the streets—might get scared and become unwilling to admit to what he has done. He may begin to argue with the young pregnant girl, claiming he is not the one responsible for her pregnancy. In a few cases, the particular young man could be right—another young man could be responsible. The problem cannot be resolved by finger pointing. The final result is the birth of another young black who follows a pattern similar to that of his or her parents.

These young black men who father babies are required by the system or the state in which they live to support the babies, but they lack the necessary education and marketable skills to obtain a good job. Or, if they do find a job, they lack the skills to develop on the job or to focus on the duties assigned. In an attempt to avoid jail or to have their driver's licenses suspended, some of these young black men will indulge in different illegal means to meet their child support obligations. An uneducated black man may be forced into illegal activities, which could lead him to jail—the very place he was initially trying to avoid.

Temika, a black girl attending public school in the Bronx, was beautiful and very intelligent, and she had planned to attend college because she was good in mathematics and science. She wanted to become an engineer or go into the military after school. Temika and her three siblings were being raised by her uneducated mother who did not have a job and was making ends meet with help from the system. The three children and Temika had never had a father at home; in fact, they were each born to different fathers. By the time Temika was fourteen, she was confiding in her friends that the house was too crowded and that she would like to get married. Even though she had been born on the wrong side of town, she was above average in her schoolwork.

Temika began to go into the streets because she wanted some of the amenities the other young women possessed, like clothes, shoes, and cosmetics, things her mother could not afford. She gravitated to Eric, a handsome black man who appeared to have money; progressive young black men from educated parents were unavailable in the streets. No one in the streets inquired where this young man, a high school dropout, was getting money. One day, Temika went to Eric and asked for money to buy a bottle of soda. He supplied the money, and their relationship began.

Temika's requests for money continued, and the kissing and hugging followed. Eric was known to be a street guy, and every young woman in the streets was seeking his attention. Temika, though fourteen years old, was telling anyone who would listen that Eric was her boyfriend. By the time Temika was sixteen, she already had a daughter. Temika followed in the footsteps of her mother and dropped out of school. She refused to name the father of her child, and Eric denied responsibility for her pregnancy since no one could prove that they had ever had sex. Society started taking care of the new mother and child. As the first child was turning three, Temika had another child, presumably by another man since no one could tell who the father of the first child was, perpetuating the lifestyle similar to that of her mother.

When Temika got pregnant, she lost her ambition to become an engineer or to join the US armed forces because she lacked the education she should have received from her parents—both as a child neglected by her parents and as a child whom society failed to step in and help. The result is a child having children. Temika, a child, was having children. What education or knowledge will Temika instill in her children? She has insufficient education to make her children recognize their opportunities or to take advantage of them.

In some cases, when both parents live with the children—which is very rare for troubled children—children are left alone to take care of themselves or one or both adults in the house is drunk or on drugs. The children could be in a worse situation by having both parents in jail. The young blacks could turn out as Temika did.

People in older generations may say that they learned and worked hard at school without the present-day scientific computers and Internet services. They are right, and they succeeded very well largely because, at the time, their grandparents, uncles, and aunts lived in the same neighborhood. That was a time when they truly believed that "it takes a village to raise a child."The villages today are multicultural. People do not trust one another. The values and norms are different today, and the new influxes do not fit in terms of culture, religion, or values. The young blacks of today do not have the extended family support that the young blacks had thirty years ago. Additionally, the media plays more of a role in exposing the ills of the society today than in the past, which makes the ills of today, like the gangs and the unwanted pregnancies, more noticeable than they were decades ago.

The extended family of the past was a great support in raising a child. The grandparents of the past were not only disciplinarians, but they inculcated the ideas of how to love and how to hug into their grandchildren. Parental support in raising children today comes from putting the kids in front of the television and computer games. As a result, children do not learn social skills or how to communicate and live with others but gain only computer gaming skills, which has little function in computer production and programming.

In some cases, young black kids are thrown into prekindergarten classrooms under the supervision of some teachers who want to be paid but would rather not be there. The free interactions among the kids are so structured in some locations that it may look like the children are in military school. The culture of the children in these schools is trending toward becoming a military culture. Unfortunately, in many states, some black kids do not have the privilege of attending prekindergarten; they remain under the supervision of a mother who may be an uneducated high school dropout with nothing to offer the child.

Based on my years of observation in the black neighborhoods, after their prekindergarten years, those young children are sent to schools that are made up of the children of middle-class, educated parents; the military-trained pre-K children; and those children from homes without proper discipline or care. The first-grade children form groups in class that are difficult for teachers to manage. The children from undisciplined home situations may lack adequate clothing and amenities, so they begin to feel inferior and antisocial and may think that they don't belong with the group from the middle-class homes. The children from the structured pre-K school begin to look at the undisciplined children as backward. The classroom becomes as divided as the society they come from.

The young black children begin to form different kinds of subgroups. The middle-class black children get called "whitish," meaning acting as white. Most children from the uneducated and undisciplined homes form their own groups and are called antisocial. A few of these children will later form gangs and drop out of school. The structured kids from the group that easily conforms are less likely to challenge the system. They are usually less inquisitive. Those from the middle-class, educated parents join the debate society and represent the school in most academic functions. The lack of self-esteem in children from the uneducated parents' group can be overcome if they excel in music, outdoor sports, or other sporting activities.

The young blacks from unprivileged and uneducated homes are more likely to continually resent the society and the system it is built on. Some children might break the mold and achieve upward mobility, but the percentages are negligible; hence, the children of a president become president. The more you invest in children, the higher the return on your investment is. So the gap between the rich and the poor gets larger. The popular saying, "The rich get richer and the poor get poorer" is true as a result of the financial investment in children.

It is highly difficult in a capitalistic society for all children to have equal opportunities because a family's wealth is greatly dependent on inheritance and education. The society can make school more accessible to children by providing their school supplies—not only the books but also the uniforms and meals. But when these male schoolchildren become adults, they will be required to register for the draft, and some will serve the nation. A few of these registered young blacks may one day serve in the armed services of the nation.

Many parents pay greatly to educate and to feed their children, including paying for their medical needs before they are required to sign up to serve the nation. Adults without children pay much less to raise the children, as parents spend as much as $240,000 before the children who serve this nation become adults. Some adults without children sometimes forget the services of the youth serving this nation and complain when required to pay school taxes. They should always be reminded that these young blacks are in the military to protect the interests of all, including the rich, in this nation. It is only fair that everyone in the nation contribute to the training of the children who serve them militarily.

A higher percentage of black kids drops out of school, just as children of presidents become presidents. The children who drop out of school will again follow the deeds and routes of their parents, and they will again start having children just as those who came before them did. In a very few cases, some of the young blacks are moved from shelter to shelter and will likely drop out of school to perpetuate the culture of dependence on the systems. However, some do escape through sports and music.

It would benefit the nation if some of the other adults without children were to contribute to the education and training of these young blacks who will be defending the nation for both the same-sex couples and the others who are less likely to have children.

# CHAPTER 2

## Environmental Influence

The environment in which people live has more effect on their behavior than genetics or any other factor of life. For example, life in the tropics encourages fewer clothes, and heating systems are not found in the homes there, unlike in the United States, where they are generally necessary. Most young blacks live in environments composed mainly of blacks either for economic reasons or for the security of being together as a result of the historical—and still existing—racial discrimination in the United States. Southwest Atlanta, Georgia, and the northeast Bronx are mainly inhabited by blacks, as is the case with Ferguson, Missouri.

Generally speaking, most poor young blacks are from poor homes located in areas usually referred to as "the other side of the railroad tracks" or ghettoes. The young blacks' parents have lived in these poor and sometimes drug-infested neighborhoods either because of racism or because they could not afford to live anywhere else. The amenities and properties of the neighborhoods are dilapidated and have little or no value. The stores in these neighborhoods are sparsely stocked with little to choose from, and the groceries that are in stock are expensive.

A child in such a neighborhood has nothing to aim for or focus on, and if he does manage to focus, his aims will be low. These detriments prevent the young blacks from having the motivation to aim high. The houses in the neighborhoods are not maintained and have low values that yield low property taxes, which in turn result in low funds for schools in the neighborhoods. The low funding makes the schools look dilapidated and allows them to fall into disrepair. In some cities, about two miles away from schools, drug dealers could be seen trying to sell drugs to men and women in luxurious cars zooming in and out of these blacks' neighborhoods. The cars that drive into these areas cost even more than the houses. Being born and growing up in these towns in the southeast of the United States, where their crop-sharing great-grandfathers lived before them, result in the young blacks' having low self-esteem and low ambition.

Many companies in these small, poor towns' neighborhoods offer low-paying jobs, such as those in warehouses and storage facilities. In such towns and villages, the young blacks are relegated to low pay. It is unfortunate that, as a result of the few jobs that also pay poorly, the easiest way to gain self-esteem and ego is for these young blacks to join gangs, become drug dealers, or resort to stealing.

A young black man passing time at a car repair shop in one of these poor neighborhoods met an influential black man who had exited the highway because of a flat tire. The young black man helped the influential man in replacing his tire. As the influential man was about to leave, he asked the young black man where he was working. The young black man responded that he did odd jobs around his neighborhood and then asked the affluent man if he could help him get a job at his workplace about five miles away. The affluent man responded to the young black man that he would try to find the young black man a job. As the affluent man turned to leave, he informed the young black man that the job required a drug test and a background check for every employee.

The young black man responded that he had done time for "taking." The affluent man questioned what he meant. The repair shop owner, who was standing nearby, responded that the act of taking was actually stealing, according to the law. Everyone present was shocked that stealing had been watered down to be called "taking." The affluent man's desire to help the young black man was dashed not only because the young black man had a record but also because he had called stealing "taking." The young blacks had belittled the act of stealing by calling it "taking." This type of culture of accepting the downgraded word would definitely be copied by the younger and the future generations, and it would be a downward spiral for the neighborhoods.

The young blacks' neighborhoods, because of what has already been discussed in this book, become scary and very unsafe for all. This environment makes it difficult for the young blacks to function effectively at school and in the streets.

The lack of income for these young blacks makes the neighborhoods dependent on government facilities like hospitals and health centers, which are in most cases poorly staffed and poorly equipped because the people of these areas are not likely to contribute to politicians during election campaigns. The young blacks are also the most unlikely population to go to the polls to vote. The hospitals and health centers that are available are usually dilapidated, just as the neighborhood schools. The young blacks who grew up in these conditions become depressed, full of anger toward the authorities or system, and unmotivated to work hard.

These dilapidated houses are not exciting to the insurance companies, the banks, or the mortgage companies. Banks and stores do not like to establish branches in black neighborhoods for fear that gangs, drug dealers, and unemployed people might damage or destroy their facilities. The high insurance rates in these young blacks' neighborhoods are often justified by the insurance companies by the fact that they pay more in those areas because of the frequency of catastrophes. These high insurance billings tend to send the young blacks and their neighborhoods into poverty.

The non-law-abiding culture of the neighborhoods and the properties' destructions put these young blacks in confrontation with the law enforcement authorities who, in turn, put these non-law-abiding young blacks in jails. The jails become a revolving door for the criminal elements of the area. The young blacks' environments of violence lead to a lack of unity among the blacks, and since unity is needed to fight large industrial and hazardous polluting companies, such plants are built in their neighborhoods.

As these companies contaminate the air, the water, and the soil, the residents tend to need to go to their doctors and hospitals more frequently than people who live in average neighborhoods. The sickness and poor health lead to absences from work, for those few who work. Some companies' executives—especially of the industries located in the poor neighborhoods—continuously try to abolish the Environmental Protection Agency (EPA), quiet their state representatives, or reduce their effectiveness so that they can continuously pollute the air, the water, and the soil of the neighborhood and the nation. The young black loses time at work, which eventually will lead to loss of pay and to poverty. These negative issues of unemployment, dilapidated buildings, and contaminated water and soil in the black neighborhoods bring the values of properties to less than the value of equivalent properties in white neighborhoods. The situations described above discourage the establishment of good schools and universities; in fact, they lead to a lack of good schools in the young blacks' neighborhoods, as is evident with the schools located in black neighborhoods today.

There is a very old historical black institution in the Southeast United States that served many young blacks in the past, yet it is presently having financial problems because the school is unable to attract new students due to crimes in the neighborhood. The neighborhood has been infested with drug dealers, gangs, and a constant police presence, as officers try to resolve one problem after another. The institution is presently selling some of its properties to maintain its viability as an institution of higher learning. The culture of violence around this institution in addition to other financial problems in the black neighborhood may soon force the school to close its doors for good.

The schools in these neighborhoods of fear, destruction, gangs, and drug dealers are unable to attract good teachers and instructors who wouldn't venture to enter such neighborhoods for safety reasons. This culture has deprived the neighborhoods of the much-needed good schools and instructors.

Jack, a BS degree holder, was once looking for a job in Bayshore, a Houston suburb, while living in a dilapidated area of Houston. He sent a resume to a chemical company but received no response. He complained to a friend who was working in Bayshore, and his friend advised him to obtain a post office box because his ZIP code was from the worst drug-infested area of Houston. Jack did as he suggested, opening a post office box in an affluent neighborhood the same distance from Bayshore as his residence. To Jack's surprise, he was called for an interview within two weeks. The post office ZIP codes identify where applicants are from. If young blacks are looking for a job and living in a dilapidated black neighborhood, it is advisable for them to do just as Jack did just to get an interview. If they are lucky enough to be called for an interview, it is also advisable that they leave the black neighborhood culture behind and interview as a professional.

On another occasion, Daniel, a young black man with a chemical engineering degree from the University of Texas at El Paso, was living in Houston in the 1980s, and he once called another chemical plant in Bayshore to inquire about a job published in the *Houston Chronicle*. He was asked to come in for an interview after a telephone discussion with the section manager responsible for the opening. On reaching the receptionist, he introduced himself and said that he was there for the interview. The receptionist told him that there was no chemical engineering job opening and that he was to go to the warehouse for a janitorial position. As Daniel was talking to the receptionist, he noticed a board behind her, and on it he saw the job opening posted. After five minutes of debate between the receptionist and Daniel, the section manager came out and walked Daniel to the conference room for the "interview." There was no further communication from the company after that.

Adding insult to injury, regulatory agencies and utility companies pay less urgent attention to catastrophes in these blacks' areas. In the 2014 storm disasters in the East, it was found that the black neighborhoods were the last to have their power restored. Such work was completed within twenty-four hours in the affluent neighborhoods. Some of the employees restoring the utilities were very reluctant to work during the night in the black neighborhoods for safety reasons, they claimed. The culture of young blacks has to encourage friendliness and hard work and also to support law-abiding citizens so as to change the perception of blacks as violent in these areas for the benefit of the society.

# CHAPTER 3

## Black Culture

The black culture as we know it today started in the days of slavery, when the black woman's respect for the black man was nonexistent, as it was arranged by the slave masters. White women were cultured to look up to and respect their husbands, but black women were cultured to respect the white man and not the black man. The line of authority was arranged in such a way that the head of the American society hierarchy was the white man followed by the white woman, then the black woman, and finally the black man. In many ways since then, the black woman has never respected the black man, but the white woman respects the white man. Since the end of slavery, black men have been trying to earn black women's respect, and it has been a challenge.

Young black men were unable to learn how to manage their households from their parents since their parents were also not trained by their parents on how to manage their households. That culture started by the white man is still a detriment to the black culture today. The slaves' masters also indoctrinated the black women during the slave days to be unfaithful to their husbands; the white men had affairs with the black women with impunity, disregarding their black husbands.

The black women's unfaithfulness to their men was inherited from the slave days. The same great-grandchildren of the slave masters are today complaining about the black culture. The slaves from the continent of Africa were not only deprived of their culture but their language. The black culture today was inherited from the slave culture, and the language is a combination of the various languages put together by the slaves.

The black slaves had no languages as they were never schooled or taught English or the American language. Slaves from different nations in Africa had to develop the black language to speak among themselves, and it is still in use today. It is funny today to hear a white person saying the black kids can't even speak. The language of a black child in the black neighborhoods can only be the language of the parents. French kids speak French; so also Spanish children speak Spanish. The black slave language Ebonics is a broken form of American English, and it is obviously going to be transferred from parents to their children.

What was the culture in the black community during slavery? The masters came around in the mornings and woke the slaves up by violently whipping them and shouting at them from the first thing in the morning to the time they went to bed in the evenings. The women were violently dragged out of the homes to serve the slave masters. Violence was the only culture they knew. Blacks who were caught trying to escape to freedom were chained and whipped until they were subdued or broken, as if they were horses. This culture of violence was certainly carried down the line of the children.

The black culture is violent today, with crimes of blacks on blacks exceeding the crimes of blacks on other races or the crimes of other ethnicities on their own kinds. Many young blacks have never been proficient in the use of words or good at expressing themselves, not only because they lack knowledge of the proper English language but also because the schools in their neighborhoods lack the funding for adequate English language instructions.

Let it be known that poverty, lack of jobs, lack of education, and lack of self-esteem—which together result in a lack of hope and failure to elevate oneself from poverty—do create depression, hatred, and anger in any man. In an environment where guns and knives are a rite of passage, the above condition unresolved could easily lead to violence, killing, and the destruction of neighborhoods. A lot of people would say that violence is a black culture, but this violence is found in many poor and deprived environments and mainly in areas with large congregations of poor people, irrespective of race. Violence of this nature has been observed in the poor areas of England, France, and the West Bank.

There is a subculture in black society, as well as in white society, in which children are having children. These children of illiteracy who lack education are unable to realize that having children will lead to poverty, even though it gives them a temporary adulthood status in addition to temporary financial security through their receiving benefits from the government. At the same time, some privately get child support from the fathers of their children. Because this situation happens frequently, some young black men end up supporting three or more households before they reach the age of twenty, as could be supported by the teenage pregnancy statistics, while youth of the same age of other races are still in college. A look at the 2010 Centers for Disease Control and Prevention's National Center for Health Statistics reveals that the teenage pregnancy rate for all races in America is 34.4 per 1,000 teens—for whites, it is 23.5 per 1,000 teens, and for blacks, it is 51.5 per 1,000. This behavior continuously keeps the young blacks in poverty.

During the slave days, some black women were forced to be

mistresses to the white slave masters, but they did not recognize them as wives and left them to be the heads of their own households. Even the present Internal Revenue Service has a grouping called "head of household."

The women-to-viable-men ratio has made it easy for men to leave a wife for another. This has been known to have led some men to marry several times to different women after divorcing their previous wives, but it is not limited to young black men; it also applies to whites. Whites are generally richer than blacks because of inheritance and education, and they are better at managing two or three residences of children. The American definition of marriage of "one man to one woman" is an adopted culture for the blacks, who are descendants of the slaves imported to this nation from the continent of Africa. There, it had become innate and genetically ingrained that polygamy not only unified the family but helped society greatly by combining resources. Polygamy also reduced the women-to-viable-men ratio. Viable men are economically stable men who are capable of providing for their youth and family.

It has also become a trend in the ghetto and black neighborhoods to call other blacks who put education first "whitish." Teaching young blacks the importance of education and the proper use of the English language could eradicate such statements, encourage education, and improve their chances of escaping poverty. Music and sports have become idealized as the easiest ways to escape poverty for many. This is actually a misrepresentation because, out of ten thousand children, one might make it into professional sports or music. What happens to the other 9,999? They are disappointed because they failed to apply themselves in school or work while they were envisioning themselves becoming sport professionals. Schools and parents should stress the importance of education to the children while they are involved in music and sports. It can be said that sports and music do not actually provide the young blacks a way out of poverty but have actually kept many in it.

Most black women do want children, and it is unfortunate that there are more women in America than viable men. The common saying by the old majority is that marriage comes before having children. Do the mathematics. If one man marries one wife, how many women, based on the women-to-viable-men ratio, will not get married? It appears a lot of women will not. Definitely some of the unmarried women would like to get married. Some men will divorce one wife to marry another and then repeat the scenario several times, and at the end of the day, a large number of the women and children will have no father figure in the house. The preaching of marrying before having children becomes unrealistic since there is a limited time range within which a woman can get pregnant.

Young blacks have a tendency to not take care of the nonconsumer goods they have. James, a barber, related that an elderly black man at his barber shop once said that the slaves never owned any landed property and that the value of nonconsumer goods was new to the descendants of slaves. Most of the descendants of slaves were looking for ways to find a peaceful environment far away from the racists and the KKKs of the nation. Although it is generally accepted that KKKs were in the South, many pockets of them were all over the country dressed in suits instead of sheets. Owning property made the descendants of slaves the envy of the KKKs and the racists of the nation. It was easier to enjoy consumer goods than to own homes that were likely to be burnt down by the KKK or taken away by discriminatory and unfair taxes or the unfair zoning of the neighborhoods.

Daniel, a retired black man, has paid off his house's mortgage, and he depends on only his retirement and his Social Security income. He paid property taxes on his house for over thirty years, and he is very likely to lose that house for failure or the inability to pay property taxes in his old age. It would be nice for retirees to not have to pay property taxes since they have paid them for years so as to keep them in their homes instead of their having to move to the Caribbean Islands south of the US border.

In the movie *Mississippi Burning*, there was a saying used: "If you aren't better than a black, who could you, be better than?" And in a play with the late actor Richard Pryor, Pryor was asked by a white man, "Why do you black people always hold your thing?" Pryor responded, "Because you have taken everything else."

Until recently, a typical black in the country could not get enough peace of mind or settle down enough to achieve wealth. It is therefore a cultural phenomenon that young blacks do not own properties or know how to maintain them. Numerous citizens of this nation still speak out against minorities moving into their neighborhoods, and other still have crosses burnt on their lawns or "KKK" written on their homes or cars. However, young blacks have started to own, develop, and maintain homes.

It is funny to think that old homes sold to young blacks were sold at higher prices than the initial purchase price when the whites were still living in the areas in the name of appreciation. As the whites move out, it usually results in depreciation. If a young black is buying a house, he should make sure that the house will not depreciate after the whites have moved out. Of what value is it to buy a house? There is very limited value or reason for the young blacks to own houses in the poor and dilapidated areas, but blacks are resented in the affluent white areas because of their race. A Brookings Institution study in 2001 found that even when home-owners had similar incomes, black-owned homes were valued at 18 percentage points less than white-owned homes. In 2007, a study by George Washington University sociology professor Gregory D. Squires found that whites reported that they would be unlikely to purchase a home that met their requirements in terms of price, number of rooms, and other characteristics in a neighborhood with good schools and low crime rates if there were a substantial representation of African Americans.

Looking at Atlanta in the fifties and sixties, the white population started moving to the suburbs. As they did, the values of the houses dropped, as did the values of the other land properties. As this book goes to print, the whites are moving back into the city of Atlanta and are buying these houses at the depressed prices. As more white families move to the city, the properties' values are beginning to rise even without repairs being made to the houses.

It is quite clear why owning properties in these dilapidated areas and in the active areas of the KKK is not beneficial to the young blacks. However, it is a good idea for a young black man to buy a house in a predominantly white area if his family is capable of dealing with some racial discrimination at the restaurants and groceries, including his children at the schools. Then and only then, his property value will rise just as for those in the white neighborhoods. Despite all the obstacles named above, the young blacks should feel pride in their ownership of properties.

The blacks moving out of predominantly black neighborhoods and living among other races will make it difficult for the system and businesses to target blacks by neighborhood and by ZIP code. The young blacks should develop a culture of honesty and of pride while at the same time enhancing their lives with good education and the proper use of the English language.

Black men used to be known to be well dressed, wearing cleaned, well-ironed clothes, with their hair kept clean and their shoes well polished. Many men and women went to "the shoe shine" for polishing in the past, keeping themselves looking sharp. They were also well respected, as evidenced by the musicians of the sixties and the churchgoers of the past. That proper dressing should be encouraged now so that the young black is respected at all times. Appearances determine how men and women are treated and respected.

## DISCRIMINATORY LAWS AND THE LAWS' ENFORCEMENTS

The good governance of a society greatly depends on its laws and their interpretations. It also depends on the citizens' perception of the laws and the interpretations they make of them. When the society members perceive the laws of the land as unfair and unjust, they are unlikely to obey the laws, the police, and other enforcers of the laws. In our society, most of the representatives who make the laws are white, and most of the laws are made and interpreted based on their life experiences, not on those of the blacks in the society.

Any rational citizen who looks at the prisons and jails in this country will wonder why the minorities, including blacks, make up the majority in these facilities. The above reasons are enough to show that the laws and their interpretations are not fairly serving the blacks in this society. Most blacks, including the author of this book, think that blacks have little input into the making of the laws and that their views are not addressed when the laws are made. The governors' offices and the statehouses of most states are occupied by whites, a situation that minimizes the blacks' concerns both in the federal and state governments. The whites make the laws of the land, and their enforcement is based on their concerns and how the laws affect them.

Critics argue that everyone has the right to vote, but there have to be incentives to vote. Blacks have to know that candidates will address their concerns. The two-party system in most situations provides two candidates of the same white race and background who have no interest in black concerns, as has been demonstrated in the conservative states in the nation. Another common criticism is, "Why don't you blacks run for office?" Unfortunately, the constant redistricting of the voting districts marginalizes blacks and gives the party in power an unfair advantage.

Blacks know this; hence, they make comments such as, "Both candidates are the same. No need to waste my gas and time." Knowing that their concerns would be addressed would be an incentive to vote. Lives were lost many years ago so that blacks could vote. Blacks have to vote for the better of two unwanted candidates *because* lives were lost for their right to vote. The fiftieth anniversary of the march on Selma for the right to vote recently took place, and it was great. More has to be done legally by the nation to get minorities into federal and state governments, as well as local government offices, so that their concerns can be addressed.

The public transportation service in Atlanta, Georgia, was not allowed to expand to certain nearby counties many years ago as it was being built because the residents of these counties thought that their comfort zones were going to be invaded by the blacks of Atlanta. The people of suburbia are the ones who control the statehouses and the governors' houses. How does anyone expect the blacks' concerns to be brought to the table and addressed in the assemblies of the nation and of the states? It is very easy to make laws while sitting in the house assemblies where everyone is happy and too content with their lives to be worried about the concerns of the blacks who live paycheck to paycheck and, worst of all, who have no food to feed their children and families.

Is there any man in America who can go home unable to feed his children and still feel happy? The lawmakers should know that a hungry and angry man is not likely to respect the laws. To address the failure of the police and of law enforcement in general is to address the root of the young blacks' unhappiness.

Those who enforce the laws that minorities have deemed unacceptable face resistance from those minorities; they have not bought into the laws and were not a part of the law-making body. One of the reasons that the fight for this nation's independence started was that the British were making laws for the people of the colonies. That is the way the majority of the blacks view the laws of this nation; they are just slightly better than the Jim Crow laws of the Southern states in the past. The "stand your ground" law in Florida and some other states is like the laws of the Wild West, and it is quite obvious that it was selectively applied in Florida in the case of Trayvon Martin. A young black man was just walking in the street in a free country, and another man, not a police officer, started questioning him. Is it legal to question his freedom of movement?

It is said that this country is a nation of law, but this fails to recognize that the interpretation of the law differs from time to time and from state to state. The interpretation of the law also differs from county to county, much less from one judge to another. The rich acquire legal services or publicity and could go as far as the Supreme Court. The legal defense groups, on the other hand, are poorly funded, and in most cases the poor are not properly defended. Many young blacks are advised to plead guilty for crimes they never committed in order to avoid jail by the legal defense groups, and the young blacks now have criminal records.

The worst legal detriments facing the young blacks are the law enforcement agencies and their employees, including the police and the sheriffs' deputies. The police and the deputies walk around the neighborhoods without smiling, looking so mean that even the babies begin to cry just by looking at them. The officers in the black neighborhoods are not representative of the population of the towns and counties. An example of this was the Rodney King riots that resulted in an overhaul of the entire Los Angeles police force. This was also the case in Ferguson, Missouri. In some forces, the police officers live in the suburbs but act as if they are mercenaries to the cities. This condition existed in Ferguson, Missouri, and in many cities in Georgia.

In the wake of Ferguson, the US Department of Justice released a report showing that drivers were essentially being taxed through traffic tickets; this was not new to most blacks. In the early 2000s, a man named James was driving on I-45 from Houston to Dallas to see a friend. He was driving at sixty-five miles per hour, but he was stopped by a sheriff's deputy and accused of driving seventy-five miles per hour. He tried to explain that he had been driving at only sixty-five miles per hour, but the police officer gave James the ticket and drove away. An innocent young black man was just made a criminal. James paid the fine and swore he would never like any police officer. That one bad police officer destroyed the young black man's trust and created hate in him for a long time. The one police officer created a monster for police officers who would encounter him in the future.

David, a student in a school in Alabama, traveled to Houston in 1979 and was stopped by a police officer for having an Alabama license plate. David explained that he was visiting Houston. Two days later as he passed the same street, the same officer kept driving behind him slowly, and David, noticing him, got worried and became nervous and scared. He unknowingly failed to stop for a stop sign. He had been harassed for almost five blocks until he was intimidated into violating a law. He was given a ticket, and then the police officer left laughing.

This money-making process in towns and cities is common in all states to keep the nonviable towns and cities functioning. The state and local governments pride themselves on not raising taxes, but they get their funding from the poor young blacks in the form of ticket fines and court costs.

The Department of Justice should not only oversee but investigate many towns', cities', and counties' enforcement agencies on a regular basis.

# CHAPTER 4

## Schools

Many people seem to think that education and literacy are the same. That is a wrong assumption because educated people are usually knowledgeable in many aspects of life, while literacy is the ability to read and write. Some family farmers or other people who work on farms and have less than a high school diploma may not be literate but are highly educated and economically efficient at managing their farms. Literacy, however, does help educated people effectively express themselves.

Though the slaves were deprived of a formal education in writing and reading, some of them secretly taught themselves how to read and write. Lives were lost by past generations in the process of earning the young blacks the opportunity to read and write. In some developing countries and Arab countries like Afghanistan and some parts of Pakistan, young women are still not allowed to go to school. In others, when children were allowed to go to school, they had to walk distances of more than five miles to get there and were still eager to attend.

With all of these difficulties and hindrances in other nations, the children of this nation, especially the young blacks, still refuse to go to school or see fit to drop out of school despite the fact that they are provided with transportation. The values and purposes for the young black to go to school should be made known to him early in his life. Just as shoes and a ball are bought for a kid to play with, each child should also be provided with reading and writing materials. Young black kids should be encouraged to read and write just as they are introduced to sports and religion.

Most young black children's parents were not educated enough to know the value of education or to direct these kids prior to going to school. It is pleasing to know now that many politicians are allocating more funds to the preschool programs in some states, including Georgia, and realizing the value of children's starting school earlier. This will be a good beginning for young blacks, just as it is with children of other races in the nation.

Some citizens do not think it is fair for the government to get involved in these young kids' education. But if these young blacks are employed in good professions when grown up, they will enhance the GDP (Gross Domestic Product) and contribute more to the Social Security fund not only for adults without children but also for those in same-sex marriages since the federal government spends these funds as they are collected. But because the young blacks are not contributing much to Social Security now, the fund is running out of money. Many could say that everyone is presently contributing to the education of the nation's children. The amount coming from the government is significantly less than the approximately $240,000 that parents will spend to grow a child to adulthood. These young adults are required to register for the draft and could be called upon to serve this nation when needed. Every member of the society benefits from the service rendered to this nation by these young men and women. It is fair and justifiable for all the citizens of this nation to help develop the young adults irrespective of the adults' marital status or decision to have children or not.

The nation's involvement in the education of young blacks does not replace the greatly needed parental involvement in their children's education. Some black parents are educated and could be perfectly right to be involved in their children's education, and those who are not educated could also be involved in many ways, such as attending the parent-teacher meetings, showing interest in the kids' discussions about school, and also making it possible for the children to receive tutorial help when needed. In the long run, the children will realize that their parents are interested in their education and schooling. It also helps the children when all the necessities for school are provided by their parents on time.

Some of the neighborhood schools are infested with drug dealers in cities like Chicago, and it is difficult for children to go to school. In Chicago and many other cities' schools, drugs are being sold on the way to school, and the gang members are operating on roads leading to the schools. In a society in which some children are afraid of bugs like spiders and bees, it is quite obvious that they would be afraid of passing a drug dealer on their way to school. Then, after school, these children are expected to find their way home. One of the kids who attended President Obama's inauguration was reported to have been shot on her way home from school. The bus drivers and the teachers are also scared of these schools' neighborhoods. It is unfair to call the schools learning institutions when, most of the time, the children are afraid of going home after school. Most people complain that inner-city schools are not doing well. Is any adult able to work effectively in such a neighborhood?

This nation sometimes protects the rich and their investments seriously but has yet to realize that their children are a national investment, and not only for their parents. This nation, the United

States, was protecting the children of Iraq on their way to school and later the children of Afghanistan on their way to school when the children of Chicago were being killed on their way to school. Society should provide adequate security and a safe environment for children to go to school by clearing the areas of drug dealers and gangs as Mayor David Dinkins did in New York, and Mayor Rudolph Giuliani later followed suit.

"Fix your house before you fix your neighbor's." The shooting of children on their way to school could be resolved by fewer than one thousand National Guard troops in a radius of a mile around most schools in Chicago. The presence of policemen or paid security officers around the schools would not only deter the drug dealers of the area but also provide a safer environment in which the children could learn. Most government buildings and government offices are guarded, and identification cards are checked before people are allowed in. How many servicemen are making sure children get to school safely in Afghanistan? How much money are the servicemen in Afghanistan costing taxpayers in this nation? Many cities would be happy for a safer environment to be provided for the children in most inner-city schools of this nation.

Two meals are served in most schools daily, breakfast and lunch. Some children from dysfunctional homes eat only at school because their parents have no food at home; some of them live in shelters. To really address the issue of having well-fed children at school is to have the other children-related agencies, like those involved in social welfare, become involved in visiting more below-average students at home to determine whether they are well fed, and teachers should also be encouraged to visit more homes during the school year.

It is typical for children from poor homes to feel inferior to kids from more affluent homes, and this does greatly affect the self-esteem of the poor children. To limit these effects, it would be better if uniforms were encouraged or made compulsory for all children in the school. It would also be better if the uniforms were supplied to the children just as books are supplied. Uniforms like those worn by most private schools, including Woodward Academy in an Atlanta suburb and most Catholic schools in New York, increase the children's self-esteem, and self-esteem makes the children feel that they are on a level playing field.

Adequate amenities in schools in the black neighborhoods would help to recruit quality teachers, if the safety issues around the schools were resolved first. Inadequate, undisciplined, and non-devoted teachers are discredits to the schools they serve. It is quite common that teachers who cannot get into better schools or are less dedicated may have no other alternative but to teach at schools in poor black neighborhoods.

Some teachers discourage children by telling them that they are no good in one subject or another. These types of teachers should be sent for additional training or disallowed from teaching. If a child gets a failing grade, the teacher certainly has a part to play and should evaluate his or her teaching methods.

# CHAPTER 5

## Higher Education

Most media and government agencies often remind the citizens of this nation that college-educated citizens earn far more than those who do not attend college or obtain a college degree. They should say in the same breath that it takes a college education for young blacks to obtain any job at all. The newspapers keep reporting that unemployment among young blacks is twice as high as that of young whites. Based on these statements, young blacks have to obtain a higher education to compete with whites who have a high school diploma. If this statement is inaccurate, why then is the unemployment rate of young black men twice that of their white counterparts?

Before a young black person or anyone else can go to college, the preparation must have begun years earlier in high school. A prospective college student has been focused for years and started working hard during middle school or at least high school to make him- or herself college material. In New York, some young black schoolchildren are not informed by their parents, their teachers, or their clergy of the importance of preparing early or of doing particularly well in certain subjects to be admitted into college or to succeed in college. Maybe some of these parents and families do not know the prerequisites for the different programs in college.

As a result of this lack of preparation, a large proportion of young black high school graduates join the armed services. Some of them who could be admitted to college choose to join the services as well because of the promised benefits, such as a paid college education and the other veterans' benefits awaiting them after their service. Both those who are qualified to attend college and those who are not look forward to these promised military service benefits. Some young blacks do actually benefit from their service to the nation if they have the necessary qualifications to go to college and if they can get a job to be able to qualify for a VA home loan; an income is required to qualify for any loan.

Attending college alone does not guarantee a job afterward. Courses or programs taken in college are of different degrees of difficulty, and their rewards after college are proportional to the work required. As indicated earlier, the courses taken in high school determine the programs that children could be prepared for in college. Educated parents and some teachers do encourage high school children to take all courses in high school seriously, and a well-prepared child has the opportunity to take any program he or she chooses in college. It is unrewarding for a child to choose courses in high school instead of taking many courses that will then allow the child to choose from a variety of programs in college.

The United States is a capitalist society that allows a choice in the type of the institution a student would like to attend. The highly ranked schools are also the most expensive and most competitive. In addition to variations in price, there are also variations in the schools' academic standards. The quality of the school also varies with the price and location. In a capitalist society, you get what you pay for.

However, many state institutions of high quality are subsidized with taxpayer money for the general public who could meet the schools' academic requirements. Young blacks who could not meet the admission requirements of these four-year colleges could choose to attend two-year colleges subsidized by taxpayers, thereby reducing the financial cost to the students.

There are also historical black colleges and universities that are eager to admit young blacks. Unfortunately, most of these schools are private and cost a great deal more than the state schools. Young blacks should be financially savvy in choosing a higher education institution. The accumulation of a hundred-thousand-dollar loan to obtain an undergraduate degree is financially unwise, and the student is likely going to have a negative return on his or her investment. If a school categorized as one of the Historical Black Colleges and Universities (HBCU) awards a young black person a scholarship, it would be wise to take it, but it must be negotiated for a four-year program. It is better to attend a state school than to take a one-year scholarship that is renewable every year after the first year. The student in most cases will have to pay the last two or three years on loan or leave college.

Student loans are lifetime loans and cannot be discharged as other loans. Students should be very careful about obtaining any student loans. Young black students should try at all costs to avoid obtaining student loans because filing for bankruptcy will not eliminate that debt. It is unfortunate that anyone can declare bankruptcy to avoid paying their car bills or mortgages, but student loans are exempt. The loans are backed by the government, which means that students could lose everything until they are completely paid.

The banks influence the government to make it impossible for students to declare bankruptcy on student loans. The universities and colleges continue to increase tuitions and other fees because they are aware that students are coming to college on federally guaranteed student loans. The government is also aware that the students will pay the loans or else Uncle Sam will beat their doors down at work or at home and at their banks to get the money. It is irrational to think that college tuitions are based on supply and demand without risk; this is not so. The schools are guaranteed by the government to get the students, and the banks are guaranteed by the government to get the payments. What a racket has been put in place by the system, and what a rip-off it is for the students.

To avoid student loans, a lot of parents try to save for their children's college funds. This is a good idea for well-to-do blacks, but for the majority who are trying to make ends meet, it is highly difficult to save for both a college fund and retirement. Some young parents build up their children's educational funds for college early and live from day to day trying to pay their monthly bills or pay the mortgage on the house that is on the verge of foreclosure. This type of life greatly affects the self-confidence of their children and may affect their self-esteem and grades at school. It is better for a young black to have a retirement investment like deferred compensation (also called 457) than to save money for children's education twenty years before they are ready for college. The money in the deferred compensation can lead to self-confidence and stability, and the saver can also borrow against it in the event that a child gets sick or ready to go to college. The funds saved explicitly for a college education cannot be used for other purposes.

The money packed away in a 457 account serves more purposes than the money reserved for children's education. The confidence that the young black has because of the 457 savings enhances his and his children's confidence, and they are more likely to do better at school. Lack of security and self-confidence are usually two important reasons that children from poor homes fail to do well in school. Some children can be rebellious at school to compensate for the lack of stability and confidence at home.

The programs that a student takes in college determine the student's path and the demand for the student after graduation. College-bound young adults should inquire from colleges of interest what percentages of their graduates find jobs within the first six months after college in the field of their study. Every freshman should have the option of one or two programs of interest. The students should be prepared to change programs in the event that their first choice ceases to be marketable or profitable. Every young black should take courses that will allow him or her to be adaptable and at the same time take advantage of other opportunities that come along in life.

# CHAPTER 6

## Financial Management

Financial management is learned or taught, and it's greatly enhanced by experience. Young blacks are just starting to learn the use and management of money. Most do not know or realize how to make money. It is a common saying in British cultures that "opportunity is all around the corner, and all that is needed is to stretch your hand and grab it." By the same token, it is believed that you just go out there and make money. The British saying forgot to state that someone has to be cultivated to recognize an opportunity before he or she will know to stretch out a hand to grab it. The same goes for recognizing money—a person has to know where and how to make it before he or she can manage the money.

The inability to recognize the value of money leads to the squandering and misuse of it. Most young blacks in this country come from homes that included slaves 150 years ago. They have never had money, and knowledge of how to manage money did not come from their parents. After the slaves were freed in this country, many became sharecroppers with little or no skill in knowing how to negotiate their deals. The others went north to work in factories at the time that employees were not unionized. The pay was low.

Both the freed slaves who remained in the South and those who went to the North were still in slavery in the form of economic slavery. Many factories still operate the same way today. Hence, it's presently taking an act of government to raise the minimum wage. Some politicians say that the marketplace should determine the minimum wage, but if that were allowed to happen, wages would have gone up at the same rate that the income of the top "1 percent" of income earners went up. When there were no minimum wages, these slaves had no increase, yet the 1 percent was getting richer. The marketplace works on supply and demand, and if the labor keeps coming from the southern border or Asia, there will be no shortage in labor for the worker to demand more pay. The supply-and-demand rule is always there, but it won't work because of the constant supply of labor. The minimum wage earner is easily replaced by the laborer from the southern border or Asia.

It is common to teach children in school the denominations of American money but not the use or management of money. Money management should be an important part of instruction in schools. Parents and churches should be eager and directly involved in teaching young blacks the value and use of money. A normal young black man would ask how and where he could get some money to manage and to save if his income will cover only half of the amount needed to pay for the rent and the food. This is not too far from reality, as will be demonstrated below.

The rich and the 1 percent group would say that they have worked minimum wage jobs and could save and go to college. It could be true, but they failed to say that they lived in their parents' homes at the time. Unfortunately, some of the young blacks are not in their parents' homes because their parents have no homes, if they were lucky enough to have been raised by them.

It is hard to say that a minimum wage of $10.00 per hour, which is equal to $400.00 per week, will cover transportation, food, and shelter in places like New York, Los Angeles, and Chicago after the deductions for Social Security, medical insurance, income tax, and the sales tax in some states like New York actually designed to tax the poor again and more, based on tax-to-income ratio. Without any of the deductions specified, the monthly income for the minimum wage earner is $1,600.00. Is there any house decent enough in New York City or any other major city in the United States that such a person can live in based on the cost of living in an apartment starting from $1,500.00 a month? Just imagine the amount left for the minimum wage earner after those deductions and the above 7 percent or 8 percent sales tax. Young blacks should not be discouraged but should be taught why education in a profitable and enduring career should be a priority before leaving high school.

John was a gentleman from Nigeria, an African nation, and was working and living in Harlem in Manhattan, New York. He wrote to his parents that he had no money and that his weekly pay was $250.00 before taxes. The parents made a budget for him based on their experience and exposure on the cost of living in their home country. In his father's letter to him, the father advised him to spend about $30.00 for rent per week, $25.00 for food per week, and $10.00 per week for clothes, and he sent him an additional $50.00. He also advised him to refuse to pay the taxes because he was not a citizen. The 1 percent group thinks just like these parents in an African country when it comes to how the minimum wage earners should manage and invest their money; it could also be said that they are ignorant of the plight of the young blacks as well.

Young blacks would be able to invest if their parents had left them some inheritance. Unfortunately, only a few young blacks have any inheritance because when this nation was being conquered and divided just like the West or being bought up for pennies, the ancestors of the young blacks were still in bondage as slaves. Where are their forty acres and a mule?

The Brentwood subdivision in Covington, Georgia, is built on fifty-five acres of land bought from Mr. Brown, a white gentleman. Mr. Brown inherited the land from his grandfather. One of Mr. Brown's two sons, Justin, was a friend and a classmate to Jeff McHenry, a black child who lived in one of the houses in the new subdivision. Justin was cutting classes one day, and Jeff was trying to do the same. Mr. McHenry told Jeff to stop roaming the streets with Justin because Justin was already aware of the definite inheritance of old money he would get from his family. McHenry told Jeff that the only way for him to get out of poverty was through education and hard work.

It is really sad to see young blacks passing through the revolving doors of the prisons instead of through the revolving doors of Ivy League institutions or other prominent colleges in the nation. This imprisonment does not enhance the disposable income of the young blacks that could be managed or invested.

During good economic times of about 5 percent unemployment, many young blacks do make money that should be properly managed or invested. Some use their disposable income to buy lots of expensive, depreciable consumer goods instead of investing the money in appreciable long-term investment goods. This is where the lack of financial training plays a role. These young blacks are eager to tell their neighbors that they are well paid on the job instead of quietly investing the money in properties or retirement funds. The communities, schools, and churches should educate these young black people on how to invest their money instead of the mega churches in the black neighborhoods.

Comedian Richard Pryor, recalling how he used to spend about six hundred dollars per day for drugs, once said, "I would have bought me Peru for the amount of cocaine I used and had me some properties, dumbass me." It is the same scenario if an employee or a young black person buys consumer goods to show that he has money. Before someone buys something, the first question to ask is why he or she needs it. In other words, why does he need a car? Is it for ego, or is it to go from Point A to Point B? Which car will safely and economically do the job? Does he want the car to attract the girls, or does he want it to inform others in the neighborhood that he has money? Also, in buying a pair of shoes, does he need the shoes for walking or to protect his feet against hazards or the weather? Does he need the shoes to keep up with the Joneses or just for the brand name?

Why does someone need a house? Is it for tax purposes only or for ego? Is there really any benefit in buying a large or an expensive house? What is really the difference in the taxes for buying a home for two hundred thousand dollars or four hundred thousand dollars? How many people will be living in the house, and does that number justify the large space? Will anyone be sleeping in two rooms at the same time? Has the purchaser estimated the cost of cooling and heating a seven-bedroom home versus a four-bedroom home? Does the difference in taxes, mortgage interest, and insurance justify the excessive payment for the larger home? In the most recent recession in the United States, the values of homes in some states like Arizona, Florida, and Georgia dropped by as much as forty 40 percent. Paying the interest and taxes on those homes was like throwing the good money after the bad. Young blacks have to address these questions and the like before purchasing anything.

David once took his daughter, Joyce, a black track star, to purchase a pair of shoes and found two acceptable pairs. One pair was nice but was not a brand name, and the other was. The brand-name pair was eighty dollars, and the other pair was fifty dollars. Joyce requested the eighty dollar pair, but David insisted that she get the fifty dollar pair. Joyce said she would pay the difference with her monthly allowance. That statement alone made David conclude that it was time for them to leave the store without any shoes. Today, Joyce is buying only cash-on-delivery used cars and saying her goal is to retire at fifty, if not earlier.

Two cousins lived in a neighborhood in the North Bronx of New York; one was Dale, an only child, and the other was Arthur, who had two siblings. It was difficult for the mother of the three siblings to buy her children brand-name goods, while the mother with only one child continuously bought him only brand-name goods. The mother of three insisted that her kids go to school with what they had. One day, Arthur got into a fight with Dale, who was teasing him for not wearing fancier clothes. Arthur told Dale to wear his shirt inside out to show the label to anyone who passed by. These days, the only son of the woman who was getting the brand-name goods is still getting them from her today while he's in jail, and the teased kid is a college graduate with his own car, living in his own apartment. The act of buying brand-name clothes alone did not lead one child to independence and the other to jail, but it shows that learning discipline and respect for others and their properties does lead to humility and respect for the law. Arrogance without control can lead to a lack of respect for others and for the law, which is the shortest path to jail.

A young black woman, Lala, working as a live-in nanny for a wealthy lawyer in Manhattan for four hundred dollars a week, walked into the store of a rich white man, who also owned the homes on the entire block of a street in New York. Lala was shopping for a dress for a function at which her employer was to receive an award. She bought a three-hundred-dollar dress for the function, where she was expected to be in a separate room watching the kids. After the function, Lala went back to the store, which was her usual weekend routine, happy that she had been the best-dressed lady at the function. When she left the store, the people there looked at one another and shook their heads, and someone said, "What was she thinking?" She had just spent three hundred dollars of her four-hundred-dollar weekly pay for a dress to wear to a function to which she was not invited and in which she did not take part. This young black woman had misplaced her priorities, as do many other young blacks who dig themselves into debt and poverty.

Analyzing every purchase a young black person tries to make is the only way he or she can make sound economic decisions and guarantee his or her exit from poverty. Unfortunately, economic education is what the young blacks lack.

The economy of this country is consumer driven, and it is painful that the young blacks support it greatly without any benefit. How many young blacks have stock in these businesses? Some have never heard of investments or owning a bank account, if they are lucky enough to have banks in their neighborhoods. Many banks are happy to put them in expensive cars and give them Christmas loans at above-average interest rates, justifying the rates with the fact that they have poor credit scores.

Post office ZIP codes were initially assigned to facilitate the movement of letters, but they are occasionally used by the banks, mortgage companies, and insurance companies to determine insurance rates for vehicles, cars, and homes. This is a form of discrimination against minorities in accessing rates.

With the recent recession in this nation, young blacks are not only the last to be hired but also the first to be let go. Many will not agree with this statement, but the high unemployment rate of young blacks is its justification. The lack of a job is a very justifiable reason for not having money and for not being a good money manager. To become good money managers, young blacks must have money to manage.

Many politicians and talk show hosts are out there complaining that the present-day young blacks do not know American history, but the general public thinks that young blacks need education in finance and in the banking system in order to acquire more of a share in the American dream.

The Affordable Care Act may provide young blacks with the health care they need to avoid tardiness and absenteeism on the job, which reduces income as well as job security. The Affordable Care Act also provides young blacks the opportunity to become entrepreneurs since they no longer depend on their employers' health insurance.

Sammy, a middle-aged black man, opened a business in New York and was on the verge of making it and of quitting his government job to be independent, but his wife, who depended on him, took ill. Sammy was unable to afford private insurance for his family, so for the sake of his wife and children, he stayed with his government job in order to keep his medical insurance. This scenario makes it obvious that the Affordable Care Act, which is available to all, has given independence to present employees, including the young blacks, to strike out and become independent business owners. It liberates them from their employers, who had their employees medically dependent on them. Young blacks need not only economic freedom but also medical insurance freedom from their employers.

# C H A P T E R 7

## Life Choices

It is common for young blacks to blame everyone and everything below the sun for their financial impediments. Society is aware that there are obstacles in place that prevent young blacks from excelling, but let it be known that the obstacles before some of the young blacks are there because of life choices the young blacks have made.

Young blacks should be told, "Each man is the architect of his own fortune." The situations of some young blacks start from birth mainly because their teenage parents are not trained or developed enough to render the young children adequate parental care. Being from low-income parents and most likely from the poor neighborhoods that result from their 15 percent unemployment rate in the inner cities of the United States, young blacks are certainly going to aim as low as the unemployed adults around them.

Tasha was a single mother with two children living in Tuscaloosa, Alabama, and dependent on social benefits. She woke up late every morning, even when her children were expected to be in class early. Tasha called on the children, telling them to wake up and go to school while she was still in bed. The children sometimes dressed and went to school while their mother was still in bed. At other times, the children stayed in bed. They emulated their mother, thereby aiming low. Adults are expected to teach by example.

When young blacks are in school, some of them gravitate to easier programs that take less time to complete or programs that require less time and less effort. Evidence of blacks' gravitation to easy programs was written by Jesse Washington and posted on STEM—Science, Technology, Engineering and Math—which said that in 2011 only 1 percent of blacks earned science degrees and 4 percent earned degrees in math and statistics. Blacks are hovering around 20 percent of the population. The reasons that Washington cited for the low levels of degree attainment in STEM fields were a) self-defeating perception that STEM is too hard, b) a lack of role models and mentors for young blacks, c) pressure to earn quick money, and d) discouraging environments. The courses involving science, technology, engineering, and math were taught in high school with memorization instead of curiosity. Math and science are not talked about at home, at the sports bar, or at the hair salon. They don't fit into the black social idea of status. Some children who are good in the sciences have been told that they could be good doctors if they devoted the necessary time and energy. "Oh my God, that is a program that takes a lifetime," many reply. "I don't need more than two years for college. In that program, you have to be in class all day and study all day as well. I need a life, and that program is not for me." Let it be known that perseverance brings success. The environment that encourages immediate gratification in life wants results now and not tomorrow.

Young blacks do not apply the maximum dedication needed to the few short programs that they take. Lack of dedication in most cases is a result of not focusing on the job at hand and claiming that they are good at multitasking. *Multitasking* is the word used by most who lack focus. This does not mean that everyone should be physicians, but young blacks should know that wealth comes from hard work, dedication, and perseverance. The reward from a career depends on the degree of difficulty of the job, just as it is with gymnastics. When young blacks play sports, they are more likely to be focused and dedicated. Sports are good for the soul and mind, but young blacks should be encouraged to focus on other endeavors as well.

Young blacks look to professional athletes as role models, but they should look to other successful members of the society as well, like doctors, bankers, congressmen, engineers, and others. Everyone cannot be a professional athlete, so they should have a fallback program after the days of athletics are over. A good education will lead to an admirable position in the society just as the athletes. A good education should go hand in hand with sports for the young blacks.

Drugs and alcohol are rampant in blacks' neighborhoods, almost on every corner. It is unfortunate that these young blacks who have never left their areas are being arrested for drugs while the major drug dealers who fly them into the country are in five-star hotels drinking together. Young blacks should resist the sales of drugs. It is very easy to say so, but the government should prosecute those who fly the drugs into the country. If the country can prevent terrorists from flying into this nation, drug dealers could also be prevented if the will is there.

Alcohol or liquor stores are rampant in the black neighborhoods, just as funeral homes are. But drugs and alcohol lead to irrational reasoning. Irrational thinking does lead to violence and may result in killing. The more killings there are in the blacks' neighborhoods, the better the business for the funeral homes. The use of alcohol and drugs is detrimental to the young blacks' neighborhoods and should be greatly discouraged by the communities, the churches, and the parents. They are the most destructive products in the blacks' neighborhoods and are getting the young blacks in jails. The use of alcohol, drugs, and cigarettes in the blacks' neighborhoods lead not only to immediate loss of focus and direction but also to long-term lung and liver issues as a result of poor life choices.

Most of the young blacks think they are invulnerable to health issues and are very likely to be unemployed. Since most of affordable medical insurance options are tied to jobs, the outcome is low pay and poverty. The poor program choices lead to low pay, which leads to a low retirement fund. In some cases, when the young blacks make a lot of money, there is a tendency to spend the money on expensive consumer goods while saving very little or nothing for retirement.

The choices made in life are significant to the life that the young black will live or enjoy in his old age; hence the British saying, "Make hay while the sun shines."

# CHAPTER 8

## Capitalism and Fairness

Capitalistic societies all over the world are the most progressive economically, and it appears in general that the standards of living are also higher. Unfortunately, comparing the nations of Western Europe and North America, it is observed that the societies with the highest standard of living also have the highest percentage of people below the poverty line. They are also the societies with the longest weekly working hours.

The disparities between the children of the affluent and the poor in the United States are also the greatest. These disparities are so great that the children of the poor live in worlds separate from those of the children of the rich, despite living in the same country. These societies have the children of presidents becoming presidents and the children of gardeners becoming gardeners. You have in America Vice President Gore's father being a senator and the Bushes, which started with Senator Bush and led to President Bush and President Bush II—maybe even President Bush III. Let's not forget the Kennedys, the Carters, the Nunns, and the Pauls. All are either politicians or eager to be prominent ones, and if they are not on the national stage, they are active in their respective states. The rich have more to invest in their children, unlike the young blacks; so the children of the rich are more likely to be presidents, and the young blacks, with little to invest in their children, are less likely to have rich children. This nation has more than three hundred million people; why does it have to recycle these same names for presidents? Let's not forget the Cuomos of New York. Capitalism is the closest system to the class system of India. Some critics will say that children often follow in the footsteps of their parents, neglecting to recognize that it takes funding to become a president and lots of money to establish a quality business. Watching CNBC's *Shark Tank* justifies numerous entrepreneurs' efforts in searching for funds to grow their businesses even after spending hundreds of thousands of dollars doing just that.

There are a few exceptions to this, but the only way to avoid the unfairness as described is to have as equal of an opportunity as is possible for the children of this nation. The children of the rich in the United States go to highly affluent schools with the best amenities, while the children in the poor areas hardly have transportation to school. The schools that the children of the poor attend are lined on all sides by drug dealers.

Many of the young adults in this nation have served in the armed services to protect the old money, which is not presently taxed, and the new money, which is. That is taxing income instead of taxing all funds. The young black servicemen are not only protecting these funds but the financial system that is in place.

Since both the old money and the new money are being protected, should they both be taxed every year? Not yet, because those with the old money and a few that are super rich rule the system and are likely to unfairly protect their funds. To be fair, the system should tax all money because protecting the financial system means protecting all money.

When the young blacks who did not go into military service are able to enter college, they are riddled with debt by both the not-for-profit and the for-profit institutions. After they get the below-standard education, the black students are unable to find adequate jobs and work, but they still have to pay for the loans with income from their low-paying jobs. As I mentioned earlier, the banks influence the government to make it impossible for students to declare bankruptcy on student loans, and the universities and colleges continue to increase tuitions and other fees because they are aware that students are paying for college with federally guaranteed student loans.

Furthermore, there is an income tax, a sales tax, a Social Security tax, and a capital gains tax, with numerous loopholes for the rich to avoid paying them. One example is a rich employee's use of a company vehicle for the entire year, which gets written off as a tax deduction. Young blacks have to pay for their transportation from their incomes.

There is wealth or money that is not being taxed, protected for the rich by the system. Recently, taxpayers paid heavily to stabilize the financial market and keep the status quo of making the rich richer by preventing an economic meltdown. What does a poor young black person lose if the market melts down? He has nothing to lose because he has no money in savings, he has no inheritance, and since he is living on a monthly income, he has no money in the stock market or an IRA. The rich will lose the billions they have in stock, IRAs, and other funds. This wealth is never taxed except for the gains earned in a particular year, while the poor young black has nothing that is not taxed. Yet some politicians refuse to give the poor a break in their only wealth, called income. The wealthy should be taxed on all their resources—not just capital gains but all capital. Are we talking of capitalism and fairness?

The rich could borrow millions from the bank, but the average student can borrow only about forty-five thousand dollars. The millionaire can discharge millions of dollars in loans, while the poor student is unable to discharge even a dollar of his loan. Are we talking about fairness?

Black students' loan amounts should be limited, not to exceed 150 percent of the amount needed to complete a four-year degree in the particular school the student is attending. That gives the student, at most, six years to finish a four-year program. The duration for a student to use a loan should also not exceed six years for a four-year degree program. Numerous students depend on this loan money to maintain their lifestyles and could remain in school for over ten years, accumulating over eighty thousand dollars of student loan debt. After the program is completed, if the student is able, he or she is faced with monthly student loan payments that exceed what many pay for their mortgages. What are the students actually losing? The nation is losing the students who are in debt, and the banks that are not going to be paid are also losing.

The young blacks see a home as an asset, as a saving for the future, and also a place to raise their children. Credit scores are the recorded histories of everyone in this nation and are consulted when someone seeks to buy a house or obtain a car loan. The credit score reporting could in some cases be good for the business communities, but many young blacks see this as another way of discriminating against them. You need good credit to obtain a loan, or you have to get a cosigner. Who will cosign for a young black without a parent or one who does have a parent without credit? The life starting point continues to move forward, and he is forced to start life late. The three credit score companies' scores are usually different. Which agencies see that these scoring bodies operate without discrimination? Two people with the same credit scores can have two different interest rates to finance their homes. The mortgage payments are usually all interest initially. Why shouldn't the developer build cheaper homes that could be financed for ten years or less? There might not be enough profit in the form of interest for the developers and the banks. Could this be regarded as discrimination or capitalism and fairness?

After the houses have depreciated and the whites return to the area, the banks and the mortgage companies begin to sing that the values of the same houses have gone up even though nothing is being done to them. The interest rates for the young blacks are usually higher than those of the whites, even if they have equal credit scores. When questioned, some banks would say that the property in the black neighborhoods is different. That is capitalism peppered with fairness.

Turning our attention to medical insurance, when someone is sick, it is easiest to go to the nearest doctor at the time. But the insurance companies would say they are not responsible for paying the bill from an out-of-network doctor.

One young black man paid to see his doctor to get high blood pressure pills. He also paid for his prescription. The doctor prescribed the specific pills for his use and they worked, but after three months, the young black man needed a refill and had to see the doctor again. Would it have been better to go to the pharmacy without having to go to the doctor first some of the time or when the patient's health has not changed? In some nations, that would have been the case. The patient ends up going to the doctor who gave him the prescription again to get the same pills. He has to pay to the doctor a tribute before going to the pharmacy. The politicians would say that the medication has to be regulated to save the weak. The politicians should stop baby-sitting all and allow evolution to control nature.

The greatest uncertainty in the capitalistic society is the way the Federal Reserve Bank manipulates the interest rate so as not to allow the stock market to collapse. By doing so, the system is just trying to keep the wealth of the rich and famous safe. Consider the scenario of allowing the stock market to collapse. It would allow everyone to start from zero. Then, the natural law of survival of the fittest would be in effect, not the survival of the old money earned or accumulated before and after slavery.

Society is easily indoctrinated, just as the young blacks are. Think of the numerous holidays in a year that pressure the young blacks to spend their money and serve to make the haves richer. Many young blacks spend the three months after Christmas paying the debt they accumulated buying Christmas gifts, when they could have been focusing on dining and bonding with their families during Christmas. Thanksgiving, however, is about celebrating with the family by getting together, eating, and bonding. At the end of it, no one is in debt, and no one bought a lousy gift or offended any member of the family because of a cheap gift. The common greeting during Christmas is, "Have a merry Christmas." Nothing could be more pleasing. Young blacks should make every day Mother's Day. They should help mothers whenever they need help, not only on Mother's Day. It is funny to send a card to a mother whose phone calls were not returned over the last six months and who was not visited when hospitalized. So also is a young black man living in his father's house, sitting in front of the computer, and failing to help him with the yard work but purchasing a card for him on Father's Day. Those presents and cards are encouraged just for economic reasons. The young blacks should save some of that money so that they can own some shares of the companies that make the cards, the shoes, the clothes, and the rest.

Pat, a young black clothing retail clerk who once worked in a Jewish clothing store in New York City, was surprised to see the amount of money the store made during the Christmas holidays. The following year, Pat opened his own store about a mile away from the Jewish store. To Pat's surprise, some of the same black customers at the Jewish store were also visiting his store. Instead of paying the marked price, as they did in the Jewish store, they began trying to negotiate the prices of the goods, which Pat did not allow. He was disappointed in his own people and could see why people talk about black-on-black destruction.

# CHAPTER 9

## Black-on-Black Destruction

Black-on-black wars are not limited to any section of this nation. They are as common in Atlanta as they are in New York, Chicago, Washington DC, Philadelphia and all other areas with a high concentration of blacks. Though the statisticians agree that crimes by blacks on blacks have increased substantially in the past fifty years based on the incarceration rate of young blacks in the prisons and jails today compared to the past, actions are yet to be taken either by the government or by the black leaders. Many blacks, young and old, in the 1960s were friendly enough to gather peacefully in order to march for equal rights and voting rights. In this gang-infested culture of young blacks today, would such gatherings and marches be as peaceful as in the past? Certainly not; rival black gangs and some undisciplined individuals would have been shooting at one another and also at the police, as recently happened in Ferguson, Missouri, and in Brooklyn, New York. Where do these gang members get the money and the drugs to wage these wars? Are the young blacks so greedy that they are unable to realize that the instant gratification from the drug money is destroying the present and the future of the participants, their neighborhoods, and eventually the black race? Critics might say that other races are doing the same around the world today, but this book focuses on the black race. The major international suppliers of these drugs fly in planes into this country, and they do not shoot at one another as the young blacks do.

Why are the young and old blacks of today not marching in the streets to eradicate hard drugs or legalize them? By legalizing the drugs, the dealers' high profit margin would disappear, making the drugs not worth their time. The churches and the black communities of the past fought the ills of the nation by marching and demonstrating in the streets and in their churches until they got what they wanted. All the members of a house or the citizens of a village have to be united to fight the streets. It takes a village to a raise a child, but the village has to be united. The young blacks need their villages back in order to raise children and to fight the ills of the streets.

The churches were meeting places, and the parents made sure that their black children followed them to the church. Are the young black adults going to church today? Visit the churches to find out. Mr. Woodley, an engineer raised in South Georgia, was once talking to his coworkers and stated that when he was young, children were taught how to hunt with guns and that the guns were not for hunting humans in the streets. He reiterated that fighting was done by hand and that within days, the children who had fought made peace and the friendship got better. By contrast, a dead friend is gone forever.

The difficulties encountered in implementing the Affordable Care Act are a good example indicating that the village no longer exists since no one is matching in the streets. Some states have also refused to implement the increase in Medicare attached to the

Affordable Care Act, and the villages or those deprived of Medicare are not marching in the streets. In a particular state, it was stated that almost five hundred thousand citizens—blacks, whites, and Hispanics—were deprived of this implementation because the politicians refused to do it in the name of cost. There are numerous millionaires in this particular state who refused to help the needy by agreeing to increase their taxes by less than ten dollars per paycheck. This Bible Belt state has a generous supply of churches. It is stated in many religious books, including the Bible, that if thy enemy is hungry give him food and if he is thirsty give him water as stated in Proverb 25:21. The churches, the communities, and the villages failed to march in the streets and to the governor's office to help these underprivileged citizens needing medical care.

In Houston, Texas, many years ago, a black resident alien walked from job site to job site looking for work, and in almost all cases the employers were interested in his resume until he opened his mouth. When they heard his heavy accent, he was turned down every time. He left one of the job sites thinking, *Hadn't Americans been coming to his country to help them? Had they not been sending them milk and grains the last few years?* Those acts of caring were what attracted him to this nation.

Young blacks should take a look at themselves in order to avoid being the poorest of the many races and colors of this nation. They haven't yet learned to live and work together like the young men of other races. The Jews in Israel, the United Kingdom, and the United States see themselves as one and work together politically. The young blacks from the United States, the Caribbean, South America, and Africa don't see eye to eye or think of working together. These young blacks whose ancestors were separated by force should not be reticent to talk to one another but should celebrate finding their next of kin.

For those young blacks who never knew or don't remember, the greatest supporting nation of South African segregation was the United States. Let's not forget the many civil rights leaders' contributions to the Coca-Cola boycott to bring attention to apartheid in South Africa. Let's not forget Rhodesia and southwest Africa. American blacks helped liberate those nations. Black America should rise up and be proud of the work done in liberating these nations. There is much togetherness between African blacks and American blacks to speak about during Black History Month.

The Affirmative Action laws put in place to help young blacks obtain employment as compensation for the long-term racial discrimination in this country were watered down. Young blacks were disallowed from taking their places as providers because the majority race decided to designate women as a minority. *Minority* in the English language means the smaller of two groups, but the population of women is larger than that of men in this country. The law requires a company to employ a specific number of blacks and women, so a black woman counts toward the quota both as a black person as well as a woman. As Richard Pryor once said, "Getting two for the price of one is a good thing." The black woman has two chances of being employed before the black man is given any consideration.

The discussions in this book so far are enough to justify anger and violence in anyone toward the governing system and authority. Every politician should get on board because the violence in the black neighborhoods could reach the white neighborhoods just as the rap music did. Rap music lyrics and the overall tone that started in the Bronx are now in the white neighborhoods.

It is fair to say that self-hatred is a problem and that it contributes to poverty in the black neighborhoods. Other racial and ethnic groups work together to achieve economic freedom. The Chinese, Mexicans, Indians, and people of other ethnicities and races have enough unity among them to start retail stores, construction companies, and even gardening together to benefit all. The young blacks from either coast of the Atlantic have less trust in one another and are very unlikely to cooperate in running any business. There is generally a lack of communication among the young blacks that hinders the trust necessary in creating a viable village or home. The lack of trust that has existed since the slave trade days on both sides of the Atlantic has been carried into the present-day workplace, and it is being enhanced by the culture of "divide and conquer" among tribes in Africa and individuals in the United States. With cooperation, the number of blacks running businesses in the country would be substantially higher than it is. According to *The Relevance of Reason: Business and Politics* by Mack W. Borgen, of June 25, 2013, the percentage of businesses owned by whites was 78.8, by Hispanics was 8.3, and by blacks was 7.1. Work has to be done by blacks so they can own a higher percentage of businesses in America.

The young blacks feel they have to look good to the white bosses by supplying them with negative information about their black coworkers. In short, some blacks still exhibit the characteristic of the old house slaves trying to look good to their managers or supervisors. Either because they want a promotion or for the sake of job security, the young blacks provide the white bosses with untrue or exaggerated negative information, which is never verified in order not to expose the source. Sometimes this type of information is also given to black bosses in companies and organizations that have young blacks in middle management positions, and those bosses generally react the same way as the white bosses.

Employees associated with the negative information are usually let go because of minor offenses or when there is consolidation at the corporation because of the unverified reports or accusations. The young black who is out of a job is back into poverty. The black neighborhoods are again getting poorer.

Young blacks should focus on disciplining their children and demonstrating to them a good work ethic. Some middle-class young blacks do try to send their children to so-called private schools, but these parents end up working two jobs to meet the financial obligations of those schools. The time spent at work leaves the children home alone without supervision or the parental guidance needed in the early stages of life, leading to unruly children.

Private schools are excellent for the children, but they have to be supported with parental care and discipline. It is more beneficial when parents allow their children to attend public schools and then stay home in the evenings to see to it that homework is done and that the children are not in the streets being exposed to illegal activities while the parents are at their second jobs.

Private school is not for every child, and no one should try to keep up with the Joneses. It was an ego boost to send a child to a private school in the Bronx, New York, in the 1990s. A certain kid from a particular private school started hanging out on the corners of the nearby streets selling drugs while the parents were busy. Sadly, this particular child dropped out of school because the parents were emphasizing the private school instead of being available at home to train the child. Discipline and stable homes for children are keys to successful adulthood.

What happened to the neighborhood watches of the past? Starting a neighborhood watch would help to reduce the destruction of properties and the stealing of cars and TV sets. The young blacks would not be free to destroy windows and doors to get to a black neighbor's TV set. The cost of replacing the stolen goods and the repairs for broken windows and doors will again send the young black people into poverty.

The young blacks' frequent use of words like *snitch* must have come from the criminal elements who want to protect themselves from being reported to law enforcement agencies. They want to operate without hindrance or risk of being reported to authorities. However, young blacks should depend on law enforcement agencies to protect their lives and property. Protecting what you have is one of the easiest and quickest ways out of poverty.

In some other black cultures in the past, around the 1900s, teenagers served as policemen. If a teenager can feel pain, the teenager should know that it will hurt if he inflicts pain on others. During an argument between a middle-aged storekeeper and a black teenager in the Bronx, the teenager said to the storekeeper that if he hurt the man, the only punishment he would get would be to go to juvenile court and by age twenty-one, he would have a clean slate. Any child above age fourteen should be tried as an adult.

# CHAPTER 10

## Discrimination and Racism

Discrimination and racism are innate in humans; that is to say that humans are born with these characteristics. They are in every person and every animal—hence the saying that birds of a feather flock together. Every human also exhibits animalistic behavior from time to time, and the combination of both leads to the human discriminatory and racial attitudes.

Society has to accept these facts before discrimination and racism can be discussed openly and addressed. Humans just have to learn to accept and live with one another because every animal tends to associate with its own kind. Humans are the same way. Resolving discrimination is a learning function and cannot be legalized to fruitfulness but taught. Failure to address the above issues will continue to plunge the world into cold and hot wars.

The Jewish and Egyptian wars, the Italian Wars, and the First and Second World Wars were spurred by the facts that one race believed that it was better than the others. The apartheid conditions of South Africa, American slavery, and Southern US segregation were based on the types and looks of a group of people compared to others. The ancient Roman citizens wrote that the British Isles were inhabited by barbarians.

The world is now a global market, and it has become necessary to address these attitudes of discrimination and racism. The best way to learn is by open association with people of other races of the world, thereby breaking the taboos and mistrust between humans. Racism and discrimination, as stated earlier, are innate in humans and will continue to exist, but humans have to continuously work hard to tolerate one another's ways of life in order to reduce or control racist and discriminatory responses to others.

Look at most colonial countries created in Africa, the Middle East, and Asia by the grouping of different races and cultures into one nation and at the same time dividing the traditional nations that existed before the colonies; this explains the recurring wars in those areas. Until recently, the people of Ukraine and the Russian Federation had lived together for years. As this book goes to print, the peoples of Ukraine and Russia are refusing to live together after they were allowed to express their innate feelings about each other.

To exist and be progressive in the global market, all races have to tolerate one another and learn to live together. Most nations in the world think of America as a nation of all people, and even Americans think of themselves as a nation of immigrants. Though this claim is true, many minorities feel the burdens of racism. The city of New York thinks of itself as a city of immigrants or the melting pot and is right to do so. New York City is one of the most vibrant cities in the United States because of the various ethnicities and races that call it home.

The citizens of the United States, one of the most enduring nations, have recently been trying to live together as a nation, but many still complain about the benefits given to minorities. America has benefited in sports and athletics internally and at international competitions because of its multiracial makeup.

America's place in sports was not actually achieved until the integration of sports and schools in the nation. The recently passed Affordable Care Act met the greatest resistance and got the least support from states that had resisted integration in the past. Many minorities believe this is so because of the perception that minorities might benefit from it. Unfortunately, many nonminorities are also losing out on the Affordable Care Act. Racism is still thriving in this nation and hurting all races.

It is very disappointing that many members of the majority race have yet to find anything positive about the first black president, despite the fact that the country has come out of a recession and that the president has made new rules to prevent what caused the recession and provided medical accessibility to many who have never had insurance for their households. However, some members of the majority, though unable to express themselves in public because of hostilities mainly from conservatives, were able to support him for reelection. Many minorities who work in this country in positions of authority experience the same criticism as President Obama and can relate to the constant dissatisfaction with his job.

Over 50 percent of the American people who voted for President Obama were celebrating the history that was being made at electing a black president, but some white conservatives were so unhappy that they did not show up at work for three days after the first election. Some members of Congress stated that Obama was going to be a one-term president even before he was sworn in and tested. Those who made such comments were members of the majority race. If such comments are made of the president, just imagine what will be said of the common minority in the streets. God forbid the names that are given to the underprivileged minorities who depend on social benefits.

Until all citizens of this country face the chronic disease of racism openly, the security of the nation will only be partial. Racism is alive and strong in this nation—and growing. No politician wants to talk or do anything more about it than render lip service. It will be to the benefit of white Americans to resolve racism and discrimination before they become the minority in less than thirty years from now. It is not easy to solve a racial problem from the position of a minority—ask the blacks. South Africa and Southern Rhodesia were ruled by whites before independence. The blacks took power in Southern Rhodesia, now Zimbabwe, without any negotiation about racism between the whites and the blacks. South Africa negotiated power with the blacks before the blacks came to power. A look at both countries is a good reason to resolve racism today before the whites become the minority.

The constant redistricting of the states' electorates helps politicians marginalize minorities, thereby rendering them no voice in the system of government. A government is only as good as those who manage it. Some political pundits keep saying that this nation is a country of law, but they refuse to state that the laws depend on their interpretation and who does the interpreting.

Most businesses are owned and managed by members of the majority race, who rightfully have full control of their businesses, and there is no government that can too vigorously enforce the law against discrimination. The law is ambiguous and very difficult to define in the first place since the enforcer is the majority. As a result of the lack of job security, an unenforceable law against discrimination, and an improper definition of *racism*, many minorities, including young blacks, tend to work for government agencies as protection from being the first to be laid off, as is usually the case with privately owned companies during an economic slowdown. The Irish did the same thing in New York when they were the new immigrants.

The politicians keep complaining that young blacks are unemployed, but they fail to understand the effects of racism. Congress
designated about 70 percent of the population as minorities, including white women, black women, and black men, but did not rank
them. So black men are minorities, white women are minorities,
and black women are also minorities. Assuming that a black man,
a white woman, and a black woman are equally qualified for a job,
which of these people would be hired because of their minority
status?

There are real problems, and the politicians are playing games
because they are not willing to resolve the problems confronting
the young blacks. In most cases, the white woman is the first choice
for a job, followed by the black woman, and if more openings still
exist, the young black man will get a chance, as shown by the
blacks' unemployment rate, which is usually more than twice that
of the whites. Rebecca J. Rosen wrote in *The Atlantic* on June 12,
2014, that the blacks' unemployment rate was 11.5 percent while
the whites' was 5.4 percent. On the same day, Jana Kasperkevic
wrote in *The Guardian* that the overall unemployment rate was 6.3
percent, while blacks' was 11.5 percent. The law has failed to define
the degrees to which these minorities are affected, and society has
failed to advocate for the removal of these racism bandages and cure
the chronic racial disease by associations.

Most children go to school in the school districts in which
they live. For the most part, white children go to school in white
districts, and black children go to school in black districts. Consider
how this affects children in the long run: The CEO and other managers of the only corporation in a small town in Georgia attended
the white high school in town. Many years later, two young adults,
one white and the other black, went to this corporation to apply for
a job, and during the interview, the CEO found out that the white
kid's father was a former classmate. When it comes time to offer the

job to one of these equally qualified young men, which of the two will likely get the job? There again is the peril of the young blacks. On the assumption that both were hired, who will be let go first during consolidation? Most likely, it will be the young black man. He will go back into poverty through no fault of his—only because he was born black and poor.

The young blacks are not wealthy enough to live among the white coworkers in their neighborhoods because the whites inherited wealth and can live in affluent areas. They are likely going to be the first or second generation out of desegregation and have no inheritance to aid them in living a more affluent life. It will be extremely difficult for young blacks to fit in with their coworkers.

Richard Pryor once laid out a hypothetical scenario. An officer lives in the white neighborhood, and the people there know him as Officer Thompson. He pulls over two young men one day, a white man and a black man. The young black man does not live in his neighborhood and does not know him, and he has to explain his movements, saying "I am reaching into my pocket for my license." The unknown young black man will be more likely get a traffic ticket, while the white young man living in the officer's neighborhood will likely get a warning.

Many US citizens will say there is no longer racism in this country because a black man, Barack Obama, is president of the United States. Go and ask the young blacks if there is still racism in this country. The answer may surprise you. Some black parents tell their children they have to work twice as hard as whites to achieve the same results in life. Racism is more pronounced in the way punishments are weighted against blacks. Compare the jail sentences for those caught with crack, the "poor people cocaine," to those caught with cocaine. You will clearly see racism in these laws and the assigned punishments.

Most local and state governments complain about a lack of

money for schools but are spending more for the building and management of prisons. It would definitely cost less to educate a black child than to build a jail and line the pockets of those who build and manage them. Until racism and its evils are addressed, the standard of education in this nation will continue to fall, resulting in an uneducated labor force and the loss of our status as the number one nation in the world

Finally, racism is hurting not only the minorities but the entire nation. Statistically speaking, if only 50 percent of the society is educated, only half of the society will be productive. The other half will drag the nation down to the level of third-world nations like Haiti, Liberia, Sierra Leone, and Somalia. The national GDP will also drop like those of third-world nations as well.

# CHAPTER 11

## Family Structures

Family structures have been going through evolution for centuries and continue to today. It is known that the human race is a relative of apes, and a conclusion could be drawn that there was a time when numerous women moved from cave to cave or jungle to jungle with the alpha male for protection. The Bible emphasized the marriages of Abraham, King Solomon, and King David, as well as those of the Egyptian pharaohs. These men were known to have had numerous wives and concubines who depended on them for shelter and food.

The Arabs had to put a limit of four wives on their men as an improvement on the then-existing multiple-wife standard. Unlimited marriages are still being practiced in many African nations today. In the Western world, the one-man-and-one-woman standard came to be accepted with little resistance. As women gained independence and became self-reliant, they fought to vote and their power at the ballot box greatly enhanced monogamous relationships.

Family structures also vary from nation to nation, as can be seen in the African, Arab, and Western nations of the world. The family structures are actually defined by the laws of a nation, not by the laws of nature. The law of nature is the behavior that is innate in man as well as in animals. No law of man can prohibit such action, as it is the case in the reproduction of man and animals.

Christ was asked if his disciples should obey Caesar's laws. His response in Luke 20:25 was, "Give to Caesar all that belongs to Caesar and to God all that belongs to God." Christ was saying that the laws of religion should be separate from the laws of the land; so also should the law of nature be separate from the law of the land. Sexuality is governed by the law of nature, and marriage is governed by the laws of nations.

The necessities of life led to polygamy in the Old Testament of the Bible when there were no offices available for women to work in. Every woman was forced to depend on the man who could grow crops and food for the family. In many nations today, where women are less educated and the economy is poor, women are still forced to depend on men for the necessities of life in the form of polygamy.

The young blacks transported to this nation against their will were practicing or were around people who were practicing polygamy. They were thrown into a society that claimed to adhere to monogamy. In actuality, the slaves' married masters were at the same time producing children of mixed races. It could be said, then, that marriage was governed quite different from sexuality.

With the liberation of the society, women, including black women, are able to express their sexual needs and desires, which have even led to women having children without husbands by choice. Many men have a wife and a mistress, and every citizen in this nation could name more than two politicians who were in the same situations.

Polygamy is already the order of the day in this nation without involving the community's property. The young black man and the young black woman with multiple baby fathers or multiple baby mothers should understand that the best way to raise their children is by living together and sharing resources. In the ancient days of David and Solomon, the women attached themselves to the rich in order to raise their children; today, many women depend on social benefits, which only keep them alive without providing an end to their miseries.

Most white men and affluent black men are, in most cases, able to support their mistresses and their out-of-wedlock children, but the often-unemployed young black man is not in a position to support his mistress or out-of-wedlock children. The issues of having a mistress belong to both black and white men, as exhibited by the numerous politicians and clergymen in the news in recent years.

It is a fact that for all races in America, having children out of wedlock is the norm for women of ages thirty-five and below. It is quite obvious that as the ratio increases, the stability of marriages will certainly decrease. The American society cherishes children, and many women would like to have children. What happens to the women who want children but can't find a man or a husband?

If a woman wants a child, she will certainly get it. If she can't find her own man, she will either get pregnant by a married man or break up his marriage and marry him in order to have her children. What happens to the children left behind by their fathers or the children of unwed mothers? Civilization of the present day needs to learn from the old civilization that has been tested in human understanding and endurance. The jumping father begins to move from woman to woman and leave the children to be supported by social benefits.

Most blacks would love to educate and support their children, but the unprogressive law of child support encourages vindictive women to be uncooperative with their children's fathers, and that makes it difficult for the fathers to be involved in the children's lives.

Brenda, a middle-age black woman living in Harlem in 1998, was unable to find a husband. She proceeded to have five children by five men, and the system was sending her money from these men and enabling her to live comfortably. Why should a woman want more than a man visiting her children? A single black woman in Houston was once asked by her boyfriend for marriage, and she responded, "I can do badly by myself; I don't need a man to do badly. Just pay your child support."

Two unmarried black women, each with a child, rented a four-bedroom house together and were redefining their family. These two black women shared the care of the children, helped each other pick up their kids from school, and shared baby-sitting duties. They were not in a same-sex relationship but were operating as a family. Why can't the law of the land accept this as a marriage and accord them the marriage insurance benefits and hospital visits as is the case with same-sex marriage? This arrangement is economically beneficial to those involved, and the presence of two adults in the household is good for the children. This arrangement is filling the void that having grandparents around the children filled in the past.

Who is in the bedroom to testify to the different types of marriages? In a few cases, the byproducts of marriages, children, are seen walking down the streets. Many religious organizations believed marriage was put in place for the purpose of raising children. It could be said that any group of people in a household raising children could be regarded as a family and accorded family benefits by the various governments.

It is time for the young blacks to find a way of living within the law or agitate for a change that will enhance their lifestyle and also benefit black communities everywhere. It is obvious that the black culture is different from white culture.

The laws of the land are designed for the white culture, and it is difficult for young blacks to live by them. Blacks have tried over the years to learn to live and behave like whites, but the majority of blacks have yet to find their way out of poverty and stay out of jail. Another approach is needed to address the family unit in the black communities since blacks make up less than 23 percent of the general population but more than 50 percent of the prison population.

# REFERENCES

1.  Gregory D Squires. George Washington University. A 2007 study on homeownership.
2.  Dorothy Brown, Emory University law school. Forbes leadership forum 2012. Brooking Institution.
3.  Jesse Washington. STEM- (Engineering Science Technology Math), Post Education on Huff.
4.  Marc Mauer, Ryan S King. Pew Research. Fact Tank
5.  Center for disease Control and Prevention. National Statistic Report. CDC Center for Disease Control
6.  Rebecca J Rosen. Blacks' unemployment rate 2014. The Atlantic.
7.  Drew Desilver. Black Incarceration. Pew Research. Fact Tank
8.  Jana Kesperskevic. Unemployment Rate. The Guardian.
9.  William A Darity Jr. Duke University. Salon
10. Bruce Drake. Pew Research Center. Fact Tank.
11. Beyond the numbers, Foreclosure rate. Longitudinal Survey of Youth 1979. U S Bureau of Labor Statistics.
12. Mack W. Borgen. Business ownerships. The Relevance of Reason and Politics

# AUTHOR BIOGRAPHY

Daniel Iyeks lived in the underprivileged neighborhoods of New York, Atlanta, and Houston for more than thirty years. He's earned a bachelor's degree and master's degree from two American universities and is a professional engineer.

Printed in the United States
By Bookmasters